Martha's Vineyard

Delapla THE

LONG WEE

Andrew Delaplaine

NO BUSINESS HAS PAID A SINGLE PENNY OR GIVEN
<u>ANYTHING</u> TO BE INCLUDED IN THIS BOOK.

A list of the author's other travel guides, as well as his political thrillers
and titles for children, can be found at the end of this book.

Senior Editors – **Renee & Sophie Delaplaine**
Senior Writer – **James Cubby**
Art Director – **Charles McGoldrick**

Gramercy Park Press
New York – London – Paris

Please submit corrections, additions or comments to
andrewdelaplaine@mac.com

MARTHA'S VINEYARD
The Delaplaine
Long Weekend Guide

TABLES OF CONTENTS

Chapter 1
WHY MARTHA'S VINEYARD?

The answer is simple—because there's no place quite like it anywhere in America. Yes, you might find some things in common between islands off Georgia or South Carolina, but none of them carry the same *élan* as Martha's Vineyard. The type of people—dare I say the *quality* of people?—that trek to Martha's Vineyard every summer are without doubt the best of the best. It's a little like Sag Harbor, but more of it.

Here on an island that used to be a whaling center you have what some people call "Hollywood East."

You get celebrities, yes, but also writers and academics and practically the entire East Coast Establishment intelligentsia. Conversation in the restaurants and bars always seems elevated to a fascinating level.

On all those other islands—from Pawleys Island to Catalina—people go to get away from it all. Here on Martha's Vineyard, they bring a little of what they left behind with them.

If you spend enough time here, you'll see what I mean. You just meet the most interesting people in the world.

Whether you agree with their views or not is another matter, but that's why it's fun and stimulating to talk to them.

Martha's Vineyard is broken up into 6 towns divided into the two sides of the island called Up Island and Down Island. (Though it would be more accurate for these divisions to be East Island and West Island.)

UP ISLAND TOWNS

AQUINNAH. The <u>Gay Head Lighthouse</u> is out here on the western end.

CHILMARK. Still a quaint area with charming fishing villages and boats bobbing in the water.

WEST TISBURY. Wild expanses of empty land. You'll be surprised to see there's so much of it still left. Lots of locals are fierce preservationists.

DOWN ISLAND TOWNS

EDGARTOWN. One of the oldest parts of Martha's Vineyard, herc's you'll see beautiful old homes once inhabited by the rich whaling captains.

OAK BLUFFS. Tourist Central, though I hate to put it that way. Lots of 19th Century architectural gems here, numerous shops, eateries.

VINEYARD HAVEN. The big ferry terminus is here in Vineyard Haven. Lots of great little shops.

Chapter 2
GETTING ABOUT

The island is only 7 to 8 miles from Cape Cod, and you can hop a ferry to Martha's Vineyard from Falmouth, Hyannis, Nantucket, New Bedford and Woods Hole in Massachusetts; Quonset Point in Rhode Island, Montauk on Long Island and also New York City.

Ferries from Woods Hole to Martha's Vineyard run year round. Others run seasonally. Check schedules. Full list can be found at www.mvy.com.

If you're bringing your car, you have to use the ferry at Woods Hole. Complete information at www.

vineyardferries.com. 508-477-8600. Trip runs 45 minutes.

If you're coming as a passenger from Cape Cod, it runs about an hour from Hyannis on the **Hy-Line,** www.hylinecruises.com. 800-492-8082.

From Falmouth on the **Island Queen** it takes about a half hour: www.islandqueen.com. 508-548-4800.

Once on the island, you can use the pretty efficient bus system that runs all over the place. The Martha's Vineyard Transit Authority, Edgartown, www.vineyardtransit.com - 508-693-9440.

Lots of taxis are also available.

Or you can rent bikes or scooters.

MARTHA'S VINEYARD BIKE RENTALS
One Main St, Edgartown, 800-627-2763
Email: marthas@marthasvineyardbikes.com
www.marthasvineyardbikes.com

Pick-up and delivery to any island location.

DEBETTENCOURT'S BIKE SHOP
Oak Bluffs, 508-693-0011
Mid Jun-Mid Sep. Bike and Jeep rentals

VINEYARD VEHICLES RENTALS
Beach Rd, Vineyard Haven, 508-693-1185.

Or rent a car or moped from:

A-A ISLAND AUTO RENTAL
800-627-6333, 508-696-5300
info@mvautorental.com
www.mvautorental.com
They have locations in Vineyard Haven, Oak Bluffs
and Edgartown.

Chapter 3
WHERE TO STAY

BEACH PLUM INN
50 Beach Plum Ln, Chilmark, 508-645-9454
www.beachpluminn.com
www.beachplumrestaurant.com
They only have a dozen rooms in this charming little
inn on a hill overlooking Menemsha Harbor. Superior
views in a wide vista. Lots of bright pastels are used
in the rooms. You'll love the alpacas that live on
the property. Just as attractive is the restaurant here,
also called the **Beach Plum** that has a brief menu
that changes daily. (Cucumber soup, Monkfish liver
crostini, lamb burger, roasted chicken for 2.)

CHARLOTTE INN

27 S Summer St, Edgartown, 508-627-4751
www.thecharlotteinn.com

The 20 rooms here look and feel absolutely nothing like what you're used to. Meaning that they don't feel like "hotel" rooms. They look as if you've been given a lavish guest-room in somebody's large private home. The rooms are so beautifully and painstakingly decorated. Grandfather clocks, antiques in every room, plush bedding and comforters, lots of bric-a-brac. (The quality of the furnishings probably accounts for their "no kids under 14" policy, and I don't blame them one bit.) The white clapboard house dates from 1864, and obviously belonged to a rich merchant or a whaling captain. Tall linden trees rise outside. (Those of you who know the place will be well aware the restaurant management changes here every now and then, but it's always an elegant place to dine. Get the lemon pot de crème, the lobster-guacamole starter, blue cheese and fig risotto. Also, they warn you about a strict dress code, but it's not always enforced.

THE DOCKSIDE INN

9 Circuit Ave, Oak Bluffs, 800-245-5979
www.vineyardinns.com
Only 21 rooms in this boutique style property where
everything is tastefully elegant. It's just a few feet
from the Oak Bluffs ferry terminal, and from their
wide wraparound porches, you can see boats making
their way in and out of the harbor. They have a 1956
Rolls Royce Silver Cloud they use as a courtesy car.

HARBOR VIEW HOTEL

131 N Water St, Edgartown, 508-627-7000
www.harbor-view.com
This historic property went up in 1891, and they
still have the rocking chairs on the wide porches to
prove it. Great views, personal service, open year-
round. I like the rooms in the old main building, but
they have more modern lodgings in their Governor
Mayhew Building. They also have cottages and suites

in another building. (In fact, they offer such a wide choice of lodgings you'd do well to look into them all before deciding what to book.) Has an excellent dining room and a very nice bar, **Henry's Hotel Bar**. Again, since they're open around the year, this is a perfect place to spend a romantic weekend—yes, even in the winter.

HOB KNOB
128 Main St, Edgartown, 508-627-9510
www.hobknob.com
Love the name of this charming B&B with its relaxing porches and cozy lobby with a fireplace they use in the winter. (There's a history about the name, but you'll find that out when you get here.) They offer 17 plush rooms, comfortably decorated, and not as "fuddy-duddy" as some of the other, older inns. (They also have 2 houses for rent year round, the Tilton House and Thaxter House—these houses have kitchens a gourmet would love to work in, so they make good choices if you want to cook.) They're proud to say they are an "eco-lodging," and your breakfast and afternoon tea are made with ingredients supplied by local farms. Business center services, spa treatments, fitness room, sauna & steam. They also

have a Boston Whaler you can use to go out to survey the Vineyard from the water—or go fishing.

MARTHA'S VINEYARD RESORT
111 New York Ave, Oak Bluffs, 508-693-6249
www.marthasvineyardresort.com
Has 6 nice rooms and 2 suites. The rooms are a little small and somewhat Spartan, but suitable. Very convenient to everything. Large lobby is great for meeting other guests or entertaining friends.

WINNETU OCEANSIDE RESORT
31 Dunes Rd, Edgartown, 508-310-1733
www.winnetu.com
The 54-suite Winnetu is as close as the Vineyard gets to a mega-resort, with a library, fitness center, and vast lawn outfitted with a nine-hole putting green and a turtle pond. The hotel is just a 250-yard walk from the beach.

Chapter 4
WHERE TO EAT

Many restaurants close in the winter off-season and others trim their hours. Check to make sure.

Only 2 towns allow alcohol to be sold: Edgartown and Oak Bluffs. Vineyard Haven has jumped in and now lets restaurants serve beer and wine (but no hard liquor), and then you have to have food served as well.

These are odd rules you expect in backwater counties in North Carolina, but not up here. Anyway, in the other towns, West Tisbury, Chilmark and Aquinnah, you have to BYOB.

ALCHEMY BISTRO & BAR
71 Main St, Edgartown, 508-627-9999
www.alchemyedgartown.com
CUISINE: Seafood, New American
DRINKS: Full bar
SERVING: Dinner
PRICE RANGE: $$$
This classy joint gets loud, but it's FUN. The bar

serves up inventive sophisticated specialty cocktails. Try the flash fried zucchini matchsticks. Later, go for the pan-fried halibut with crispy skin or the soft shell crabs with a cornmeal breading.

AMONG THE FLOWERS CAFÉ
17 Mayhew Ln, Edgartown, 508-627-3233
www.amongtheflowersmv.com
CUISINE: American
DRINKS: Beer & Wine Only
SERVING: Breakfast, Lunch, & Dinner
PRICE RANGE: $$
Just a block from the Edgartown harbor is this popular small café offering a menu of comfort food standards including delicious sandwiches and salads. Get a seat in the brick patio where there's plenty of shade in the summer. Great breakfast pick. Favorites include: Lobster rolls and Turkey & Swiss sandwich. Gluten-free options available.

ART CLIFF DINER

39 Beach Rd, Vineyard Haven, 508-693-1224
No Website
CUISINE: American
DRINKS: No Booze
SERVING: Breakfast, Lunch
PRICE RANGE: $$

Retro diner offering a menu of American classics. It has those old-time swivel stools at the lunch counter, and I've hated them all my life, almost as long as this place has been open, which is decades. But I put up with them because the diner food is so damn good.

ATLANTIC FISH & CHOP HOUSE

2 Main St, Edgartown, 508-627-7001
www.atlanticmv.com
CUISINE: Seafood
DRINKS: Full Bar
SERVING: Lunch, Dinner
PRICE RANGE: $$$
Casual eatery that feels more like a yacht club

(because of its lively bar scene) than a restaurant.
Great menu of steaks and seafood. Favorites include:
Tuna tartare and Lobster roll. Hangout on the second-
level deck.

THE BLACK DOG TAVERN

20 Beach St Extension, Vineyard Haven, 508-693-
9223
www.theblackdog.com
CUISINE: Seafood, American
DRINKS: Beer & Wine Only
SERVING: Breakfast (from 7), Lunch & Dinner
PRICE RANGE: $$
This is quite a place. You'll notice their logo plastered
all over the island. The inside is decorated with a
wondrous array of nautical artifacts, everything from
netting to tackle, buoys, oars—you get the idea. It's
just that there's so much of it. Sit outside at a picnic
table and take in the splendid waterfront view. You're
really here for the view. Service is spotty and the food

is OK, most especially the lobster mac & cheese, the chowders, the egg dishes in the morning.

ESPRESSO LOVE
17 Church St (behind the courthouse), Edgartown, 508-627-9211
www.espressolove.com
CUISINE: Coffee shops; Sandwiches & Salads
DRINKS: No booze
SERVING: Breakfast (from 6), lunch till 6 p.m.
PRICE RANGE: $
Great selection of fresh baked goods, good breakfast items, hearty sandwiches and entrée sized salads for lunch. But the COFFEE is a big attraction here, too. Lots of celebs show up here. But there's room for you, too. Very friendly. Christina Thornton (chef-owner of **Hooked**), starts her morning here with an iced coffee.

GIORDANO'S CLAM BAR
18 Lake Ave, Oak Bluffs, 508-693-0184
www.giosmv.com
CUISINE: Pizza
DRINKS: Full Bar
SERVING: Lunch, Dinner
PRICE RANGE: $$
Open for over 80 years, this place is known for its family style Italian classics and pizza. (The whole fried clams are a standout.) Carry-out window offers a take-away option for those looking for a quick lunch.

HOME PORT
512 N Rd, Chilmark, 508-645-2679
www.homeportmv.com
CUISINE: Seafood
DRINKS: No Booze

SERVING: Lunch, Dinner; closed Tues & Wed
PRICE RANGE: $$$
Known for its traditional seafood, this eatery also features a raw bar on the outside deck and a take-out window. Favorites include their deservedly famed clam chowder and lobster dinners.

LARSEN'S FISH MARKET

56 Basin Rd, Chilmark, 508-645-2680
www.larsensfishmarket.com
CUISINE: American
DRINKS: No Booze
SERVING: Breakfast (from 9), lunch & early dinner (till 7)
PRICE RANGE: $
In the fishing village of Menemsha. It is a great spot for clams or oysters on the half shell and to watch the

sunset. (**Menemsha Beach** is one of the few places you can actually watch the sun set into the water.) Though the big deal here is the fresh fish for sale in the market, their kitchen will cook to order these items: Lobster, Chowder of the Day, Lobster Bisque, Stuffed Quahogs, Stuffed Scallops, Crab Cakes, Steamers, Mussels. The seafood here is about an unadorned, unfancy and GOOD as you can get.

PORT HUNTER
55 Main St, Edgartown, 508-627-7747
www.theporthunter.com
CUISINE: Seafood
DRINKS: Full Bar
SERVING: Dinner
PRICE RANGE: $$S
Very friendly eatery that's so relaxed they offer tables for standing and regular seating. The décor matches the seafood-focused menu. Menu favorites include: Quinoa fritters, fish tacos, Chatham mussels in a spicy curry sauce, Buffalo Brussels sprouts served with a

blue cheese mousse. Music later. Great cocktails and shuffleboard.

RED CAT KITCHEN
14 Kennebec Ave, Oak Bluffs, 508-696-6040
www.redcatkitchen.com
CUISINE: American (New)/Seafood
DRINKS: Full Bar
SERVING: Dinner
PRICE RANGE: $$$
A very welcoming atmosphere greets you here, whether you eat inside where you can enjoy art created by locals or outside on the porch beneath the Chinese lanterns. This place offers a very creative menu with names to match. Try the Island Fresca – a Parmesan soup with island corn, tomatoes, and basil that is quite famous locally. The dishes come with a great medley of local vegetables that makes every dish special.

RIGHT FORK DINER
12 Mattakesett Way, Edgartown, 508-627-5522
www.rightforkdiner.com
CUISINE: Burgers
DRINKS: Full Bar
SERVING: Breakfast, Lunch & Dinner
PRICE RANGE: $$
Though it's on the island's southeast tip next to the Katama Airfield, people head out here for the excellent quality food—especially good for breakfast. Breakfast treats include their incredible blueberry buttermilk pancakes and homemade chocolate chip pancakes. Other favorites include the Breakfast burrito and the Lobster Cobb salad. Also good for

lunch is their PBLT, a flavorful sandwich stuffed with smoked pork belly, tomato, lettuce and aioli on a sourdough roll.

SCOTTISH BAKEHOUSE
977 State Rd, Vineyard Haven, 508-693-6633
www.scottishbakehousemv.com
CUISINE: American
DRINKS: No Booze
SERVING: Breakfast, lunch, dinner
PRICE RANGE: $$
More to this place than meets the eye. Take a look at the garden out back—a lot of the food they serve here comes from it. Egg sandwich for b'fast is only $4; full line of sandwiches for lunch, hefty wraps; entrees include quesadilla; spicy peanut noodles; Brazilian plate; kale & sweet potato mash; soups, salads, all fresh, fresh, fresh. (They go through 100 pounds of kale every week in season.) Specialty menu items for you if you're vegan, a carnivore, localvore, baconitarian, gluten free, sugar-free, you name it. Open year round.

STATE ROAD

688 State Rd, West Tisbury, 508-693-8582

www.stateroadmv.com

CUISINE: Diners

DRINKS: No Booze

SERVING: Breakfast, lunch, dinner

PRICE RANGE: $$$

The Obamas liked this place, and so will you. Try the bacon cheddar Jalapeno grits for breakfast. (Hot!) Or the hash that changes daily. Lunch from 11 till 2: sandwiches and salads. Dinner (from 5:30) offers treats like sugar snap pea salad, shrimp & grits and lobster salad for starters, and items like loin of rabbit, lamb chops or prosciutto wrapped monkfish for main courses. Very nice spot. They have gardens out back that supply lots of the ingredients served here. This is a relatively new place on the Vineyard, but it still has a "tavern" feel to it, with wood beams and rustic chandeliers giving off a cozy glow.

THE SWEET LIFE CAFE
63 Circuit Ave, Oak Bluffs, 508-696-0200
www.sweetlifemv.com
CUISINE: American
DRINKS: Full Bar
SERVING: Dinner
PRICE RANGE: $$$$
Elegant spot with prices to match in this Victorian
house offering up a romantic setting you'll love
the minute you walk in. Great tuna tartare and very
creative soups. The meats are top quality: lamb
sirloin, breaded quail breast, dry-rubbed rib eye. (You
can get seafood a hundred other places, right?) Has
one of the better wine lists on the island.

Chapter 5
WHERE TO SHOP
(& SERVICES)

ALLEN WHITING GALLERY
985 State Rd, West Tisbury, 508-693-4691
allenwhiting.com
Gallery exhibiting the work of local artist Allen
Whiting – known for his oil paintings featuring
locales in the surrounding area.

ALLEY'S GENERAL STORE

299 State Rd, West Tisbury, 508-693-0088

No Website

This wonderful place has a sign out front that says "Dealers in Almost Everything," and it's been here since 1858. It's always been a general store, so it's the kind of place where you get everything you need, kind of like an old fashioned 7-11 or convenience store. Must stop if you're in West Tisbury.

BESPOKE ABODE

56 Main St, Vineyard Haven, 508-693-0722

www.bespokeabode.com

This comfortable shop has lots of items for the home, especially if you're looking for that island feel. Interior designer Liz Stiving-Nichols chooses everything: unusual picture frames, mirrors, pillows, some furniture.

BOOK DEN EAST

71 New York Ave, Oak Bluffs, 508-687-9830

No Website

Funky used bookstore offering eclectic collections on art, Western literature and works of "local" though internationally famous writers such as David McCullough and William Styron.

CHICKEN ALLEY

38 Lagoon Pond Rd, Vineyard Haven, 508-693-2278.

No Website

Unique thrift shop that is also part art gallery. A favorite of anybody who likes funky clothing. Shelves of used books, clothing, household items, furniture, artwork and collectibles. The shop hosts the annual

Chicken Alley Art's and Collectible Sale on the 2nd Sunday in August.

THE CHILMARK COFFEE COMPANY
12 Lagemann Ln, Chilmark, 508-560-1061
chilmarkcoffeeco.com
Todd Christy has dedicated himself to creating the best coffee in the region and his coffees are sold all over the island. This is where it all starts.

CHILMARK GENERAL STORE
7 State Rd, Chilmark, 508-645-3739
www.chilmarkgeneralstore.com
An old-fashioned market is a locals' meeting place and a great stop for lunch. The market sells island-grown produce, coffee, household necessities, and almost anything that you might need. Great sandwiches and fresh organic coffee. Grab a slice of their famous pizza and eat it on the porch.

FIELD GALLERY

1050 State Rd, West Tisbury, 508-693-5595
www.fieldgallery.com

This gallery has been exhibiting the work of island artists for over 35 years and continues to feature a group of talented artists. Rotating exhibitions of contemporary paintings, sculpture, photography, and other works. Artists' receptions are held Sunday afternoons throughout the summer.

GRANARY GALLERY

636 Old Country Rd, West Tisbury, 508-693-0455
www.granarygallery.com

Not your typical gallery geared to tourists featuring "island-y" paintings by local artists. This place features high-end art, with the price tags to match—sculpture, photos, and paintings—by some 70+ big name international artists. (A few locals are represented as well.) Owners are the discerning Christopher and Sheila Morse.

MARTHA'S VINEYARD GLASSWORKS
683 State Rd, West Tisbury, 508-693-6026
www.mvglassworks.com
The glass works of 6 or 7 artists are on sale here in this fine shop, from platters to bowls, tableware, jars, vases, display pieces. Here you'll find any number of inventive pieces that will make a great addition to your home (or even your office) or as a gift.

MERMAID FARM & DAIRY
9 Middle Rd, Chilmark, 508-645-3492
www.facebook.com/Mermaid-Farm-and-Dairy-371138872899/
Founded in 1997, this 35-acre farm and dairy sells a variety of vegetables, raw milk, handmade yogurt, feta cheese, wheat and rye flours, beef, lamb and pork. Worth a visit.

MIDNIGHT FARM
44 Main St, Vineyard Haven, 508-693-1997
No Website
Very pricey upmarket place, so look for any sale
items. Expensive handbags, great children's clothing,
unusual furniture. Carly Simon is one of the owners.
Has that Anthropologie feel, only much better. Even
if you're on a budget, come to this place when the
weather's bad. You'll love just browsing.

NORTH TABOR FARM
4 North Tabor Farm Rd, Chilmark, 508-645-3311.
No Website
A six-acre farm run by Rebecca Miller with a farm
stand on premises selling fresh items like salad
greens, eggs, pork, poultry, mushrooms, honey, and
flowers.

ONE HOT YOGA

7 Woodland Center, Vineyard Haven MA, 774-327-1287,

www.one-hotyoga.com

Offering a variety of yoga types including: Bikram Hot Yoga, Barkan Hot Vinyasa, Baptiste Power Vinyasa, and Sanchez/Ghosh Lineage.

TEA LANE FARM

Chilmark, 774-563-8274

tealanefarm.com

Historic farm owned by the town of Chilmark. Krishana Collins sells her gorgeous flowers at the local farmers' market. Her services are available for weddings, special events, and flower services. The beautiful farm is ideal for hiking, mountain biking and dog walking.

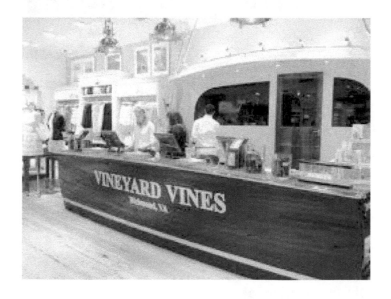

VINEYARD VINES

27 N Water St, Edgartown, 508-627-4779

www.vineyardvines.com

Great books, gifts, polo shirts, lots of gifts focusing on the Vineyard.

WEST TISBURY FARMERS MARKET

1067 State Road, West Tisbury, 508-693-9561
www.thewesttisburyfarmersmarket.com
Runs from Jun – Oct, Wed & Sat, 9 – noon, rain or
shine. The fruits and vegetables you can buy here
come from people on the Vineyard who grew them.
Lots of fun. (They also have an abbreviated winter
market.) Questions? Contact Linda Alley at 508-693-
9561, or email linda@newlanesundries.com

Chapter 6
WHAT TO SEE & DO

AQUINNAH BEACH
MOSHUP BEACH / NUDE BEACH
www.mvy.com

On the west side of the island is this nice public beach
with some parking. Here you'll get to see the cliffs of
clay, which rise straight up from the long stretch of
lonely beach. (Plan on walking.) The nude section of
the beach is at the north end.

THE CAMPGROUND
Oak Bluffs, 508-693-0525
www.mvcma.org
Email: office@mvcma.org
Here they have an organization called the Martha's
Vineyard Camp Meeting Association (MVCMA),
that is quite interesting and well worth your time
to look into. They have numerous activities and
events in the summer season. There are dozens of
Victorian gingerbread cottages. While the cottages
were ostensibly built by devout Methodists who set
up "camps" when they met here, beginning as far
back as 1835, there's been a lot of restoration. Once a
year they do a Grand Illumination (I know, it sounds
like something from another world) when they hang
colorful Japanese and Chinese lanterns in all the
cottages. (Usually in the middle of August.) Fun place
for the whole family.

CEDAR TREE NECK SANCTUARY
Vineyard Haven
www.sheriffsmeadow.org
Here you will find a lovely preserved area that
offers splendid relaxed views of forestry, a pond
and the ocean beyond. Cedar Creek is maintained
by the Sheriff's Meadow Foundation, which has an
interesting history. Over in Edgartown, Sheriff Isaiah
Pease owned a meadow that came to be known as
Sheriff's Meadow. On it there was a pond used in the
winter to cut ice for storage later in the year. Henry
Beetle Hough, the editor of the local "Vineyard
Gazette," lived nearby and his windows looked out
onto the meadow. When he heard the area was going

to be developed, he used $7,000, the advance for a book from a New York publisher, to buy the meadow and preserve it. When none of the other preservation groups wanted to take the property, he and wife Elizabeth launched the Sheriff's Meadow Foundation, which now boasts many other areas of Martha's Vineyard that will be preserved for years to come.

CHAPPAQUIDDICK

You can jump on a ferry to Chappaquiddick, which is only 300 yards off the Vineyard's east coast. Here you can enjoy miles of empty beaches (depending on the time of year and day you go). Bird watchers flock here to look at spot blue herons, sandpipers and the like.

DR. DANIEL FISHER HOUSE
99 Main St, Edgartown, 508-627-4440
www.mvpreservation.org/p.php/preservation/venues/daniel-fisher-house
Built in 1840, this Federal style residence is open for visitors and available for weddings and such.

EDGARTOWN LIGHTHOUSE
In Edgartown Harbor
www.mvmuseum.org/edgartown.php
In front of the **Harbor View Hotel**, take the path off N Water St.

FISHING WITH JENNIFER CLARKE

Chilmark, 508-645-2440

captainclarkecharters.com

Jennifer Clarke, also a successful singer/songwriter, offers a wide variety of charter fishing excursions. Climb aboard Captain Clarke's 30-foot center console charter vessel "Femme Fatale" for what I promise you will be a memorable experience. Martha's Vineyard is a fisherman's paradise boasting the best in striped bass, bluefish, bonito, false albacore, fluke and sea bass fishing.

FLYING HORSES CAROUSEL

15 Oak Bluffs Ave, Oak Bluffs, 508-693-9481

www.mvpreservation.org

Open from Easter Sunday through Columbus Day. This is one of the oldest carousels in America and a national landmark, and you just have to see it, even if you don't take a ride. Its horses were hand-carved in 1876 in New York City, one of 2 known carousels built by Charles W. F. Dare. In 1884, the Flying Horses were brought from Coney Island to Martha's Vineyard and have been operating on the same site for more than a century. Rides are cheap. (And if you catch the brass ring you can get a free ride.)

GAY HEAD LIGHTHOUSE
9 Aquinnah Circle, Aquinnah, 508-645-2300 (ext. 0)
Tues-Sat, mid-June through mid-Sept.
www.gayheadlight.org

GREAT ROCK BIGHT PRESERVE

37 Brickyard Rd, Chilmark, 508-627-7141
mvlandbank.com
Owned by the Martha's Vineyard Land bank, this
preserve is free to visit. The preserve features many
trails and access to 1,300 feet of beach along the
Vineyard Sound. The preserve is used for nature
study, hiking, picnicking, mountain-biking, horseback
riding, hunting (with permission), fishing, and
swimming.

ISLAND ALPACA

1 Head of Pond Rd, Vineyard Haven, 508-693-5554
www.islandalpaca.com
They breed alpacas here on this 20-acre farm. You can
feed the critters and take them for walks. But you'll
definitely want to visit the gift store with its clothes
for babies, footwear, handbags, totes, purses, jackets,
coats, hats, headbands sweaters, scarves, shawls—all
made of alpaca here on Martha's Vineyard.

JAWS BRIDGE

Seaview Ave, Edgartown

If you want to see what MV looked like in 1975 (and she what's changed and how much hasn't), take a look at Steven Spielberg's 1975 film, "Jaws."

The film crew descended on Edgartown with their 24-foot shark and took the place over for a few months. You'll see lots of houses, stores and other locations in the movie that are still here.

Jaws Bridge is officially the **American Legion Memorial Bridge**, but locals refer to it as **Big Bridge**. It's part of Seaview Avenue, which connects Edgartown with the town of Oak Bluffs. The bridge also divides the Atlantic Ocean from Sengekontacket Pond.

Despite its nickname, the bridge is a small one, just a few car-lengths in total, and it has been refurbished in recent years. The stone quay Roy Scheider ran during the Jaws attack at the bridge is still there and runs perpendicular to the bridge. The beach on the ocean side, called Joseph Sylvia State Beach, was where the rest of the scene was filmed.

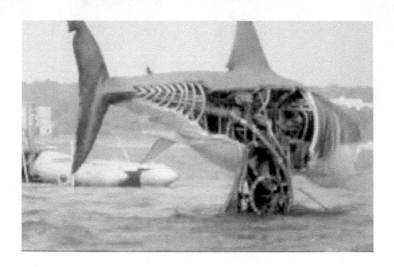

LIGHTHOUSE BEACH
Water St, Edgartown, 508-627-6145
No Website
You can get spectacular views of Chappaquiddick
from the top of this 45-foot high cast iron lighthouse
after climbing the spiral staircase. Originally built
in 1881 and installed at Ipswich, Mass., it was
taken apart and brought here after the lighthouse in
Edgartown was damaged in a hurricane.

LONG POINT WILDLIFE REFUGE
Hughe's Thumb Rd, 508-693-7392
Off the Edgartown – West Tisbury Road
www.thetrustees.org/places-to-visit/cape-cod-islands/long-point.html
Salt and freshwater ponds, hundreds of acres of
beautiful virgin beachfront. At more than 600 acres,
Long Point is one of the largest publicly accessible
properties on Martha's Vineyard. It encompasses
beach, dune, and woodland that surround a broad
(and uncommon) sand plain heath. While busy in
season, the refuge is especially fun in the winter.
(Birdwatchers love it.)

THE MARTHA'S VINEYARD MUSEUM

59 School St (Cooke & School Sts), Edgartown, 508-627-4441

www.marthasvineyardhistory.org

Authoritative source for history and genealogy on the island. Excellent exhibits including the Thomas Cooke house, the Francis Foster Museum, the Captain Francis Pease House and Carriage Shed with coverage of whaling and Wampanoag history as well. Modest admission.

MENEMSHA BEACH

Basin Rd, Chilmark

Just a couple of minutes' walk from the fishing village that gives this beach its name, you'll find perhaps the BEST sunset on Martha's Vineyard.

OLD WHALING CHURCH
89 Main St, Edgartown, 508-627-4442
www.mvpreservation.org/p.php/preservation/venues/old-whaling-church?_f=w
Built by whaling captains in 1843, this landmark is considered on of the finest examples of Greek Revival architecture in New England.

VINCENT HOUSE MUSEUM

99 A Main St, Edgartown, 508-627-8017

www.mvpreservation.org/properties/vincent-house-museum

Built in 1672, this is probably the oldest standing house on Martha's Vineyard. The museum houses furnishings that show examples of Puritan life to the more elegant Whaling era.

Chapter 7
NIGHTLIFE

Nightlife options are somewhat limited by the nature of Martha's Vineyard. In addition, only 2 towns allow alcohol to be sold: Edgartown and Oak Bluffs. Vineyard Haven has jumped in and now lets restaurants serve beer and wine (but no hard liquor), and then you have to have food served as well.

These are odd rules you expect in backwater counties in North Carolina, but not up here. Anyway, in the other towns, West Tisbury, Chilmark and Aquinnah, you have to BYOB.

Some of these are really restaurants, but because they have a lively bar scene, I've put them here to "create" a nightlife" section.

20BYNINE
16 Kennebec Ave, Oak Bluffs, 508-338-2065
www.20bynine.com
CUISINE: American (New)
DRINKS: Full Bar
SERVING: Dinner nightly, Sunday Brunch
PRICE RANGE: $$
This gastropub is known for its wide selection of American whiskeys—and the bartenders know how to make creative cocktails using them. It's also a friendly eatery that offers a menu of high quality food created from seasonal ingredients. Menu favorites include: Lobster fritters and Mason-jar ricotta.

THE LAMPOST

6 Circuit Ave, 508-693-4032

I love the way they handle the address on their web site: "Circuit Avenue – no number needed – look for the biggest building." And they are quite right. It boasts 4 floors with things happening everywhere. In the basement is the **Dive Bar**. Live music down here. Main floor offers a big screen TV, keno, pool tables, live music on weekends. Third floor has the biggest dance floor on the island. Live music is featured on Thursday and Friday nights with local and off island bands. Saturdays are reserved for the DJs. On the top floor is the **Lounge**, where one repairs when one wants to "get away from it all." Let's just say Martha's Vineyard would be a sadder, less lively place without the Lampost.

LOLA'S

15 Island Inn Rd, Oak Bluffs, 508-693-6093

www.lolasmv.com

CUISINE: Seafood

DRINKS: Full Bar

SERVING: Lunch, Dinner

PRICE RANGE: $$

A favorite that offers Southern classics like ribs and chicken & waffles but also fresh seafood specials. Favorites include: Fried green tomato nachos and Crispy Black bass.

Great spot for brunch. Dancing to live music (soul and R&B) on weekends, DJs on weeknights.

OFFSHORE ALE CO

30 Kennebec Ave, Oak Bluffs, 508-693-2626
www.offshoreale.com
This locals' pub is also the only brewery on Martha's Vineyard, and as easily could be in the "What To See & Do" chapter. As such, it's better as a nightlife destination, there being so few places to go here on Martha's Vineyard at night. Toss those peanut shells right on the floor. They don't care. Get the Offshore Amber Ale that's made right there on the premises.

PARK CORNER BISTRO

20 Kennebec Ave # H, Oak Bluffs, 508-696-9922
No Website
CUISINE: American
DRINKS: Full Bar
SERVING: Dinner nightly and Sunday brunch
PRICE RANGE: $$
Friendly place that offers of menu of creative American classics. Try their pop stickers to start. Great cocktails. Live music, house DJ.

RITZ CAFÉ
4 Circuit Ave, Oak Bluffs, 508-693-9851
www.theritzmv.com
On the dock you'll find this dive bar that has live music nightly during season (but off season only on weekends).

SHARKY'S CANTINA
31 Circuit Ave, Oak Bluffs, 508-693-7501
66 Upper Main St, Edgartown, 508-627-6565
www.sharkyscantina.com
They boast "50 menu items under $10," so this is a good place to bring the kids. But the bar is busy at night.

INDEX

Other Books by the Same Author

Andrew Delaplaine has written in widely varied fields: screenplays, novels (adult and juvenile), travel writing, journalism. His books are available in quality bookstores as well as all online retailers.

JACK HOUSTON / ST. CLAIR POLITICAL THRILLERS

THE KEYSTONE FILE – PART 1
THE KEYSTONE FILE – PART 2
THE KEYSTONE FILE – PART 3
THE KEYSTONE FILE – PART 4
THE KEYSTONE FILE – PART 5
THE KEYSTONE FILE – PART 6
THE KEYSTONE FILE – PART 7 *(FINAL)*

On Election night, as China and Russia mass soldiers on their common border in preparation for war, there's a tie in the Electoral College that forces the decision for President into the House of Representatives as mandated by the Constitution. The incumbent Republican President, working through his Aide for Congressional Liaison, uses the Keystone File, which contains dirt on every member of Congress, to blackmail members into supporting the Republican candidate. The action runs from Election Night in November to Inauguration Day on January 20. Jack Houston St. Clair runs a small detective agency in Miami. His father is Florida Governor Sam Houston St. Clair, the Republican candidate. While he tries to help his dad win the election, Jack also gets hired to follow up on some suspicious wire transfers involving drug smugglers, leading him to a sunken narco-sub off Key West that has $65 million in cash in its hull.

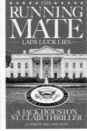

THE RUNNING MATE

Sam Houston St. Clair has been President for four long years and right now he's bogged down in a nasty fight to be re-elected. A Secret Service agent protecting the opposing candidate discovers that the candidate is sleeping with someone he shouldn't be, and tells his lifelong friend, the President's son Jack, this vital information so Jack can pass it on to help his father win the election. The candidate's wife has also found out about the clandestine affair and plots to kill the lover if her husband wins the election. Jack goes to Washington, and becomes involved in an international whirlpool of intrigue.

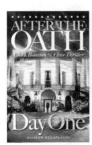

AFTER THE OATH: DAY ONE
AFTER THE OATH: MARCH WINDS
WEDDING AT THE WHITE HOUSE

Only three months have passed since Sam Houston St. Clair was sworn in as the new President, but a lot has happened. Returning from Vienna where he met with Russian and Chinese diplomats, Sam is making his way back to Flagler Hall in Miami, his first trip home since being inaugurated. Son Jack is in the midst of turmoil of his own back in Miami, dealing with various dramas, not the least of which is his increasing alienation from Babylon Fuentes and his growing attraction to the seductive Lupe Rodriguez. Fernando Pozo addresses new problems as he struggles to expand Cuba's secret operations in the U.S., made even more difficult as U.S.-Cuban relations thaw. As his father returns home, Jack knows Sam will find as much trouble at home as he did in Vienna.

THE ADVENTURES OF SHERLOCK HOLMES IV

In this series, the original Sherlock Holmes's great-great-great grandson solves crimes and mysteries in the present day, working out of the boutique hotel he owns on South Beach.

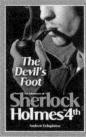

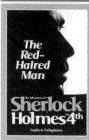
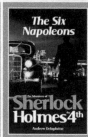
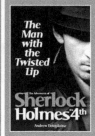

THE BOSCOMBE VALLEY MYSTERY

Sherlock Holmes and Watson are called to a remote area of Florida overlooking Lake Okeechobee to investigate a murder where all the evidence points to the victim's son as the killer. Holmes, however, is not so sure.

THE DEVIL'S FOOT

Holmes's doctor orders him to take a short holiday in Key West, and while there, Holmes is called on to look into a case in which three people involved in a Santería ritual died with no explanation.

THE CLEVER ONE

A former nun who, while still very devout, has renounced her vows so that she could "find a life, and possibly love, in the real world." She comes to Holmes in hopes that he can find out what happened to the man who promised to marry her, but mysteriously disappeared moments before their wedding.

THE COPPER BEECHES

A nanny reaches out to Sherlock Holmes seeking his advice on whether she should take a new position when her prospective employer has demanded that she cut her hair as part of the job.

THE RED-HAIRED MAN

A man with a shock of red hair calls on Sherlock Holmes to solve the mystery of the Red-haired League.

THE SIX NAPOLEONS

Inspector Lestrade calls on Holmes to help him figure out why a madman would go around Miami breaking into homes and businesses to destroy cheap busts of the French Emperor. It all seems very insignificant to Holmes—until, of course, a murder occurs.

THE MAN WITH THE TWISTED LIP

In what seems to be the case of a missing person, Sherlock Holmes navigates his way through a maze of perplexing clues that leads him through a sinister world to a surprising conclusion.

THE BORNHOLM DIAMOND

A mysterious Swedish nobleman requests a meeting to discuss a matter of such serious importance that it may threaten the line of succession in one of the oldest royal houses in Europe.

SEVERAL TITLES IN THE DELAPLAINE SERIES OF PRE-SCHOOL READERS FOR CHILDREN

THE DELAPLAINE LONG WEEKEND TRAVEL GUIDE SERIES

Delaplaine Travel Guides represent the author's take on some of the many cities he's visited and many of which he has called home (for months or even years) during a lifetime of travel. The books are available as either ebooks or as printed books. Owing to the ease with which material can be uploaded, both the printed and ebook editions are updated 3 times a year.

Atlanta	Memphis
Austin	Mérida (Mexico)
Boston	Mexico City
Cancún (Mexico)	Miami & South Beach
Cannes	Milwaukee
Cape Cod	Myrtle Beach
Charleston	Nantucket
Chicago	Napa Valley
Clearwater – St. Petersburg	Naples & Marco Island
Fort Lauderdale	Nashville
Fort Myers & Sanibel	New Orleans
Gettysburg	Newport (R.I.)
Hamptons, The	Philadelphia
Hilton Head	Portland (Ore.)
Key West & the Florida Keys	Provincetown
Las Vegas	San Juan
Lima (Peru)	Sarasota
Louisville	Savannah
Marseille	Seattle
Martha's Vineyard	Tampa Bay

THE FOOD ENTHUSIAST'S
COMPLETE RESTAURANT GUIDES

NOTES